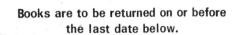

THE HUMAN BODY

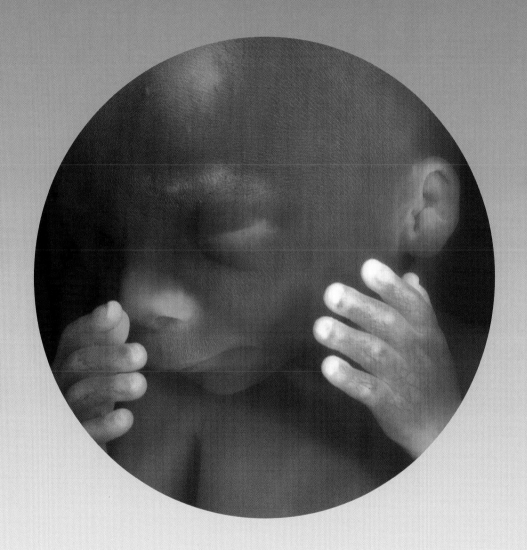

John Farndon

HODDER
Wayland

an imprint of Hodder Children's Books

SCIENCE FACT FILES

COMMUNICATIONS · CRIMINAL INVESTIGATION
THE EARTH'S RESOURCES · ELECTRICITY AND MAGNETISM
FORCES AND MOTION · GENETICS
THE HUMAN BODY · LIGHT AND SOUND
THE SOLAR SYSTEM · WEATHER

Produced by Roger Coote Publishing
Gissing's Farm, Fressingfield
Suffolk IP21 5SH

Design and Typesetting	Sarah Crouch and Victoria Webb
Commissioning Editor	Lisa Edwards
Editor	Sarah Doughty
Picture Researcher	Lynda Lines
Illustrator	Alex Pang
Text Consultant	John Stringer

Endpaper picture: A section through the cerebral cortex.
Title page picture: A fetus at 19 weeks.

We are grateful to the following for permission to reproduce photographs: Digital Vision
cover top, *endpapers*; Gettyone Stone *cover* bottom, (Nicholas Veasey), 20 top
(Michaelangelo Gratton), 25 (Sanders Nicholson), 26 (David Madison), 27 (Angela Wyant), 34
(Chad Slattery), 37 (Jon Riley); Robert Harding 33 right (Michael Lichter); Science Photo
Library *cover* main, *title page*, 9, 10 (Quest), 12 (Alfred Pasieka), 15 (Dr Jeremy Burgess), 16
(Andrew Syred), 18 (David Scharf), 20 bottom (C.C. Studio), 28 (Biophoto Associates), 30
(Tim Beddow), 33 left (Prof P. Motta/Dept. of Anatomy/University "La Sapienza", Rome), 38
(Francis Leroy, Biocosmos), 40 (Neil Bromhall), 43 (Biology Media); Still Pictures 42
(Ron Giling).

Printed in Hong Kong by Wing King Tong

A CIP catalogue record for this book is available from the British Library

ISBN 0 7502 3183 1

Hodder Children's Books
A division of Hodder Headline Ltd
338 Euston Road, London NW1 3BH

CONTENTS

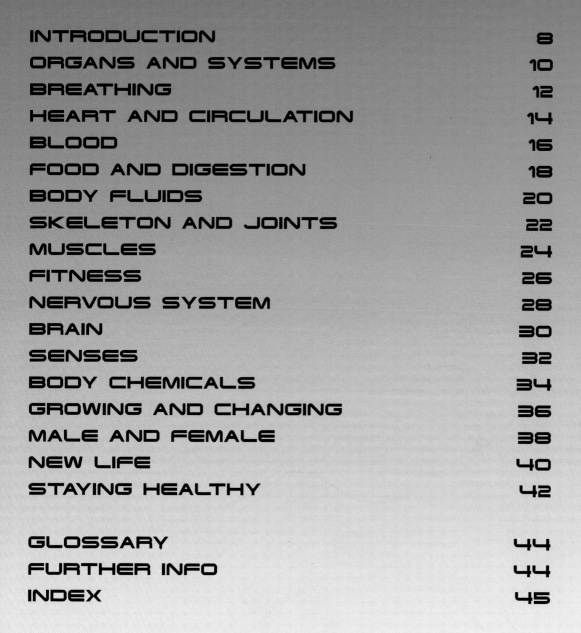

The words that are explained in the glossary are printed in **bold** the first time they are mentioned in the text.

INTRODUCTION

Every moment of the day, even while you sleep, your body is busy at work. Your chest is steadily pumping air in and out of your lungs. Your heart is squeezing powerfully away, sending blood shooting through the blood vessels. Digestive chemicals are at work in your intestines, processing food. Nerve signals are buzzing to and fro, sending information from the senses to the brain and carrying instructions to all parts of the body. Chemical messengers are coordinating all kinds of processes.

All these activities have the same purpose – to keep you alive. Just as with every living creature, from the tiniest bacteria to the biggest whale, all the many and varied bits of the human body work together to maintain its life. What is amazing is that every living creature is kept alive by many tiny living machines – living cells, the building blocks that your body is made from. Most living cells are so small that you can only see them under a powerful microscope. It would take 10,000 to cover a pinhead.

Living Cells

Your body contains over 75 trillion cells! They are all squashy cases of chemicals held together by a thin casing called the cell membrane, made of fat and protein. The membrane lets certain chemicals move in and out of the cell. Inside is watery fluid called cytoplasm, with various tiny structures, called organelles, floating in it. Near the centre of each cell of your body is the cell's nucleus, the control centre which contains the chemical instructions for all the cell's tasks. Every time a new chemical is needed, the nucleus sends the instructions to the rest of the cell.

A typical cell showing the different organelles.

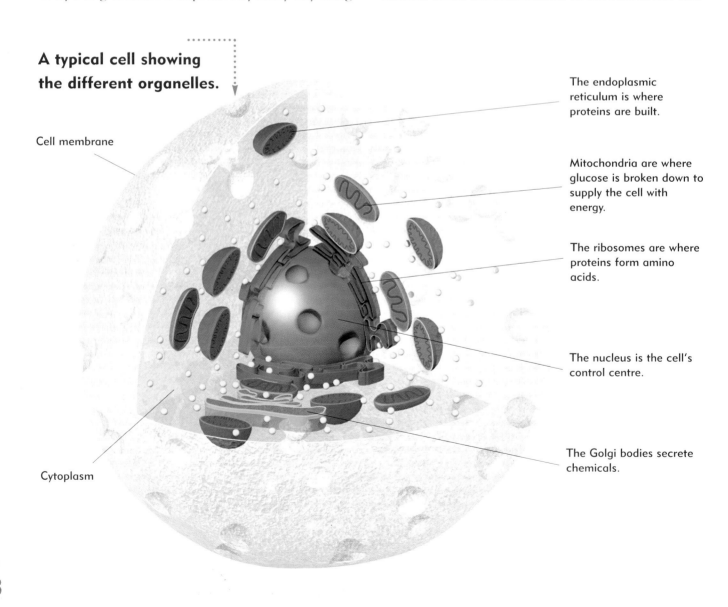

Cell membrane

Cytoplasm

The endoplasmic reticulum is where proteins are built.

Mitochondria are where glucose is broken down to supply the cell with energy.

The ribosomes are where proteins form amino acids.

The nucleus is the cell's control centre.

The Golgi bodies secrete chemicals.

REVEALING THE BODY

In the sixteenth century, Flemish physician Andreas Vesalius (1514–64), and other physicians were working at Padua in Italy. They had read the works of the ancient Roman physician, Galen, but his ideas about the workings of the human body had remained unchallenged for over a thousand years. Vesalius was a practical scientist and he and the group of physicians started obtaining and carefully dissecting dead bodies. They had detailed drawings and engravings made of everything they found. Vesalius's book *De Humani Corporis Fabrici* meaning 'what the human body is made of', produced in 1543, is the most important book about the human body ever written.

Andreas Vesalius laid the foundations of our modern knowledge of anatomy.

Cells and Tissues

While the very simplest living organisms are made of just one kind of cell, most animals are made of various different kinds of cells. Human bodies are made of over 200 different types of cells – each with their own special task. These types of cells include skin cells, liver cells and fat cells. The cells group together to make materials called tissues.

There are four basic kinds of tissue. Nerve tissue is made of identical cells called **neurons**, which are good at sending electrical signals. The skin and the walls of all the parts inside the body are made of epithelial tissue – which are various kinds of waterproof cells. Muscle tissue is made of special long, reddish cells that are able to pull shorter and then relax. Connective tissue is made of loosely packed cells that hold the muscles, nerves and epithelial tissue together. It has different forms including 'adipose tissue', better known as fat, tendons and **cartilage**. Bone and even blood are also connective tissues.

ANATOMY

Anatomy is the geography of the body. It looks at the structure of the body – where everything is and how it all fits together. When describing the human body, it is usually assumed that the body is standing upright, facing towards you, with arms hanging down by the side.
• The body is divided into two halves forming a line of symmetry down the middle (the 'median' plane).
• The body is divided into right and left.
• The body is also divided in half crossways front to back (the 'coronal plane').
• Things in front of the coronal plane are said to be anterior or ventral.
• Things behind the coronal plane are said to be posterior or dorsal.

ORGANS AND SYSTEMS

A microscope reveals the bands of special cells that make up muscle fibres.

When a house is built, bricks are put together to make walls. In the same way, cells in the body are put together to make tissues. And just as walls make up various different rooms in the house, so tissues make up various different 'organs' in the body. Organs are essentially different bits of the body with a particular role. The heart, for instance, is an organ that pumps blood round your body. The kidneys are organs that filter the body's waste water. The skin that covers you is the body's biggest single organ.

Body Systems

There is another way your body's cells work together, besides being literally stuck together to make organs and tissues. Inside the nucleus of each cell are the coded instructions which tell it to play a particular role. All these individual roles enable organs and tissues to work together to make complete systems with particular tasks – just as pumps, pipes, radiators, boilers and hot water work together to make the central heating system that keeps a house warm.

Some of the body's systems extend throughout the body, like the skeleton which is the body's framework, the musculature (muscle) system which is the body's means of moving, and the nervous system which is the body's communication network. Others are quite localized, like the digestive system, which is the body's food processor, and the excretory system which controls waste including urine. The body could not function without all of these vital systems, and they all work together to keep you alive.

THE BODY'S MAIN SYSTEMS

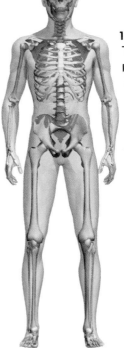

1. Skeleton, or skeletal system
The skeleton supports your body and protects internal organs such as the lungs and heart.

2. Musculature, or muscle system
The muscles are what enable you to move, and are also involved in other body systems.

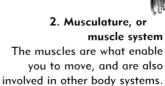

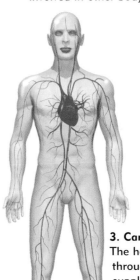

3. Cardiovascular system
The heart pumps the blood that circulates throughout your body to keep body cells supplied with oxygen and food, to carry waste away from cells and to defend the body against germs.

4. Nervous system
The nervous system is the brain, spinal cord and nerves – the body's high speed electro-chemical control network.

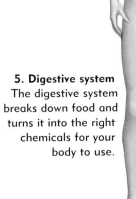

5. Digestive system
The digestive system breaks down food and turns it into the right chemicals for your body to use.

6. Immune system
The immune system is the body's various defences against disease. It includes the lymphatic system of lymph fluid which contains white blood cells and antibodies.

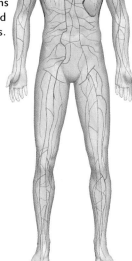

7. Reproductive system
The reproductive system is essentially the genitals and the organs connected to them – the organs that enable us to have children. This is also the only body system that can be surgically removed without threatening your life.

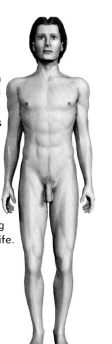

8. Hormonal system
The hormonal (or endocrine) system regulates the body's hormonal activities. It consists of the endocrine glands which produce hormones which are carried around the body.

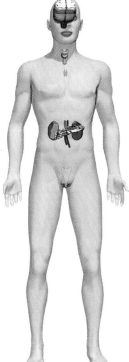

Other Body Systems Include:

9. Excretory system
The excretory system retrieves water from digested food and gets rid of solid waste and excess liquid as urine.

10. Respiratory system
The respiratory system takes air in and out of your lungs through the mouth and nose, giving oxygen to the blood and taking out carbon dioxide.

BREATHING

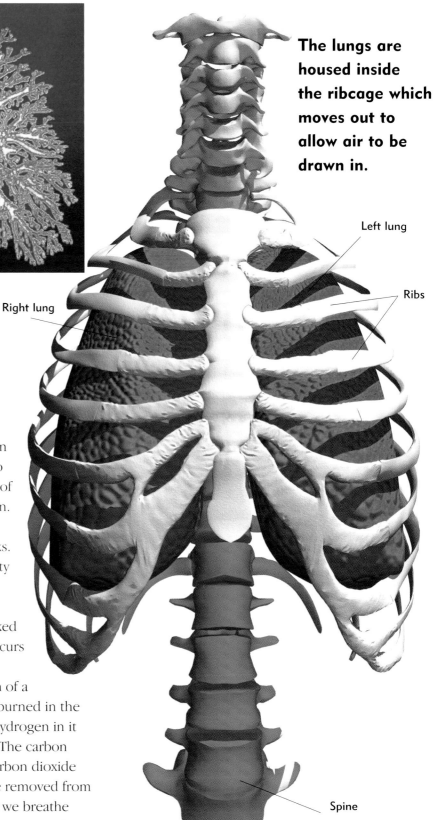

A resin cast of the airways serving the lungs, showing the branches that make up the respiratory tract.

The lungs are housed inside the ribcage which moves out to allow air to be drawn in.

Left lung

Right lung

Ribs

Spine

You have to breathe to live. When you breathe in, you take air into the body. Without this frequent intake of air, every cell would rapidly break down. Air contains the oxygen needed to sustain the cell and fuel its various tasks. Just as a fire only burns if there is plenty of air, so each cell needs oxygen to burn up the food it receives via the bloodstream to release the energy locked within it. The process by which this occurs is called cellular **respiration**.

Food arrives at the cell in the form of a sugar called glucose. When glucose is burned in the cell to release its store of energy, the hydrogen in it combines with oxygen to make water. The carbon also combines with oxygen to make carbon dioxide (see page 26). Carbon dioxide must be removed from your body. This is what happens when we breathe out. Expelling carbon dioxide is as important as the intake of oxygen; if the body becomes clogged with carbon dioxide, we die just as surely as we would if we failed to breathe in oxygen.

FACT FILE

BREATHING FACTS

- You will probably take about 600 million breaths if you live to the age of 75.
- Every minute you breathe, you take in and give out about 6 litres of air.
- A normal breath takes in about 0.4 litres of air. A deep breath can take up to 4 litres.
- On average, you breathe about 13–17 times a minute. But if you run hard, you may have to breathe up to 80 times a minute.
- Newborn babies breathe about 40 times a minute.
- Air normally contains about 21 per cent oxygen, and about 0.04 per cent carbon dioxide. The air you breathe out has about 0.6 per cent carbon dioxide.
- There are about 300 million alveoli in your lungs.
- Opened out and laid flat, the inside of the alveoli would cover an area the size of a tennis court.

The Airways

Air enters the body via the nose or mouth and is carried to the lungs. The lungs are a pair of large, greyish-pink bags in the chest, rather like two foam-rubber cushions. The lungs encase an intricate network of tubes that lead air to and from the mouth and nose. This branching network of airways, called the respiratory tract, is shaped rather like a hollow tree turned upside down.

Every time we take a breath, air rushes swiftly through the throat and into the broad trunk of the tree called the voice box. It streams over the taut ligaments of the vocal cords, and on down into the windpipe (the trachea), until it reaches a fork deep within the chest. At this fork, the airways branch into two, one branch or bronchus leading to the right lung, the other to the left lung.

Once in the lungs, the air flow gradually slows down as the airways divide and re-divide, becoming narrower each time, until it finally reaches the tiny twig-like bronchioles.

Around the end of each bronchiole are grapelike clusters of tiny air sacs called alveoli. The alveoli are the gateways for oxygen into the body. Each alveolus is encircled by a network of tiny blood vessels – like a string bag around a football. Oxygen seeps through the thin walls of the alveoli and into the surrounding blood vessels, then is carried to each of the body's cells in the bloodstream. The blood, slowing down as it squeezes through the tiny blood vessels, picks up the oxygen and bears it away to cells all over the body. Carbon dioxide passes out from the blood into the alveoli in the same way.

Air is rarely in the lungs for more than a few seconds, so this exchange must take place very quickly. This is where the tree-like shape of the respiratory tract comes in. Its branching structure covers a huge surface area – a great deal of oxygen can seep through, and an equal amount of carbon dioxide can seep back in a very short time, even though it only seeps through slowly at any one place.

The airways end in grapelike clusters of tiny sacs called alveoli.

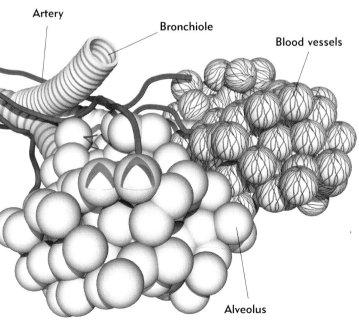

Artery

Bronchiole

Blood vessels

Alveolus

13

HEART AND CIRCULATION

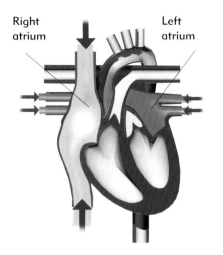

Right atrium   Left atrium

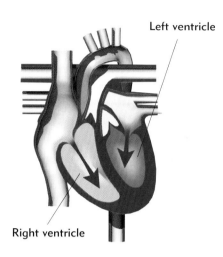

Left ventricle

Right ventricle

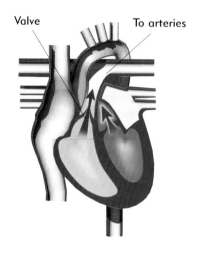

Valve   To arteries

1. Blood flows into the relaxed atria (where blood accumulates).

2. Muscle contraction sweeps across the atria pushing blood into the relaxed ventricles (the pumping chambers). Valves snap shut to hold the blood in the chamber.

3. Less than a tenth of a second later, the wave reaches the ventricles. The valves open and the ventricles contract, squeezing blood up into the arteries.

TEST FILE

FEELING YOUR PULSE

Your pulse is the tiny shock wave that runs through the blood as your heart valves snap shut. Try laying two fingertips gently on the inside of your wrist in the slight dip on the thumb side. Move your fingertips slightly around until you can feel a slight regular swelling. This is your pulse. Using a watch or clock with a second hand to time you, then count how many pulse beats there are in a minute. Repeat to see if it varies.
• Normal pulse rates vary between 50 and 100 beats a minute.
• The average pulse rate for a man is about 71; for a woman it is 80 and for a child it is about 85.
• A pulse of over 100 beats a minute is 'tachycardia'; less than 60 beats a minute is 'bradycardia'.
• Any abnormality in the pulse rate is called 'arrhythmia'.
Test your pulse after vigorous exercise, and you will probably find it is much faster than usual – sometimes up to twice as fast.

Once in the blood, oxygen must be delivered swiftly to the cells. At the same time, unwanted carbon dioxide must be collected from the cells and brought back to the lungs for breathing out. This is where the body's remarkable blood circulation system comes in. Pumped around by the heart, blood moves through an intricate network of blood vessels all the way round the body. As if on a roundabout with no exit, it circulates round again and again, once every 90 seconds. Blood rich in oxygen continually streams away from the lungs carrying this gas to every part of the body. Day and night, the circulating blood gathers unwanted carbon dioxide from the cells and brings it back to the lungs.

Double Systems

Blood circulation is split into two systems. Both systems start and finish at the heart and the two sides of the heart are its pumps. The smaller system feeds the lungs alone and is known as the pulmonary circulation. It sends oxygen-poor blood from the heart to the lungs and brings it back to the heart with fresh oxygen. The larger system is known as the systemic circulation and it feeds the rest of the body. It sends oxygen-rich blood on from the right side of the heart and carries it round the body and back to the left side of the heart.

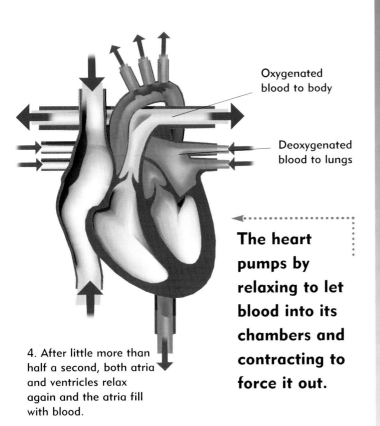

Oxygenated blood to body

Deoxygenated blood to lungs

4. After little more than half a second, both atria and ventricles relax again and the atria fill with blood.

The heart pumps by relaxing to let blood into its chambers and contracting to force it out.

Surprisingly, perhaps, oxygen is not just swept along by the blood. Instead, it is stowed safely inside hundreds of millions of tiny, button-shaped red blood cells. Each of these tiny rafts can carry a great deal of oxygen because they contain a remarkable substance called **haemoglobin**. Haemoglobin can take up oxygen when there is plenty around, yet give it up when there is a shortage. It glows bright scarlet when it is carrying oxygen, which is why blood is red. But it fades to dull purple when it loses oxygen.

Aorta

Vena cava

Femoral artery

Iliac vein

The heart pumps oxygen-rich blood to the body, and draws blood depleted of oxygen back to the lungs for a fresh supply.

HISTORY FILE

BLOOD CIRCULATION

Early in the seventeenth century, the English physician William Harvey (1578–1657) was studying the human body and trying to work out the connection between the heart and the blood. He was the first to realize that the heart was actually a pump, pushing blood around the body – again and again. Blood flow, he suggested, is a circulation. It leaves the heart via the arteries, then flows back via the veins. We now know that blood gets from the arteries to the veins via tiny blood vessels called capillaries. The tiny capillaries could not be seen until the invention of the microscope in the 1670s – but Harvey's theory of blood circulation was correct.

In the early 1600s the physician William Harvey realized that blood flow is a circulation.

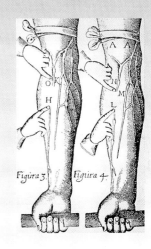

The Heart

The heart is one of the body's marvels, beating every second of our lives to keep the blood circulating. Even while we sleep, the heart goes on tirelessly pumping away, perhaps at a rate of 70 times a minute – much more when we are running about. The heart's powerful muscles contract to send great jets of blood shooting through the blood vessels.

The heart is made of a special kind of muscle called cardiac muscle. Unlike other muscle, cardiac muscle works entirely by itself without any trigger from nerves. So your heart goes on beating regularly all the time without you ever having to think about it. Even when removed from the body altogether, a heart will go on beating as long as it has blood to pump.

BLOOD

Blood is the body's transport system. It not only carries the vital oxygen supply to every single cell in the body, it also carries all the food needed to fuel and maintain the body's tissues – such as the muscles, skin and brain. It bears the chemical regulators that ensure each cell works as it should. It washes away all the unwanted material to the liver, kidneys and lungs. And it spreads heat evenly over the body to keep it at just the right temperature. What is more, blood plays a vital role in the body's defences against disease. With so many and varied tasks to perform, it is hardly surprising that it is a complex liquid.

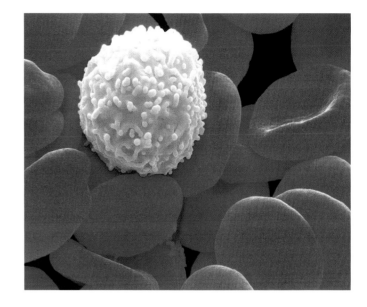

Seen through a powerful microscope are button-shaped red blood cells with a lone, small white blood cell.

BASOPHIL
Releases antibodies.

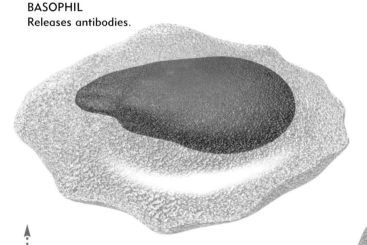

EOSINOPHIL
Releases antibodies including histamine.

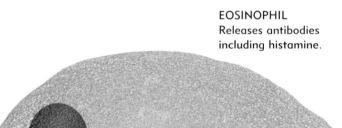

Your blood contains red cells, platelets and a range of giant white cells.

Blood Mix

Blood looks a bit like red ink. But through a powerful microscope, you can see a rich mix of different cells, bathed in a clear, yellowish fluid called plasma. And in the plasma are dissolved hundreds of different substances, such as sugar which provides the body cells with energy. Blood cells fall into three main groups. By far the most numerous are the button-shaped red blood cells that carry oxygen. Then there are the tiny irregular platelets. And finally there are giant white cells. Together, these cells make up just under half the volume of blood; the rest is plasma.

White Cells

While red blood cells carry oxygen, white blood cells help the body fight germs. Most white blood cells are filled with tiny grains and so are called granular leucocytes or granulocytes. They include the giant white cells called neutrophils which are the blood's cleaners. Their job is to swallow up any intruders and digest them in a process called phagocytosis, which simply means 'cell eating'.

The two other kinds of white blood cells release antibodies (see page 43) to help fight germs. These granulocytes are called eosinophils and basophils. Basophils store a chemical called histamine which helps draw the blood's army of defenders to any site of infection. Histamine is what makes an infection itch as it heals.

White Cells without Grains

Two kinds of white blood cells do not contain grains. Monocytes are scavenger cells that roam the blood eating up unwelcome guests. But they are real professionals, able to dispose of not only the more obvious intruders such as bacteria, but also, acting on instructions, the less obvious foreign bodies like virus-infected cells. The role of lymphocytes is not simply to eat cells for defence. One of their tasks is to help provide the instructions for the monocytes and other defence cells to identify intruders. Some lymphocytes, though, act as 'killer cells', attacking intruders directly.

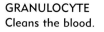
GRANULOCYTE
Cleans the blood.

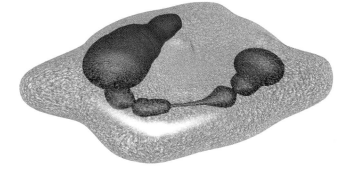

Platelets

Platelets are just chips broken off other cells as they formed. Yet they play a key role in the defence of the body by helping to plug any leak, such as a cut, to stop blood being lost. They also help to stop blood loss by releasing special clotting activators that encourage fibres to form around the wound. Blood cells get caught up in the tangle of fibres and form a clot that plugs a leak.

FACT FILE

BLOOD FACTS
- A person weighing 80 kg has 5 litres of blood.
- A child weighing 40 kg has 2.5 litres of blood.
- 0.5 litres of blood plasma is replaced in 2 hours if you give blood.
- There are 5,000,000 red blood cells in every cubic millimetre of blood.
- Red blood cells live for 5 months.
- 1.5 million new blood cells are produced in the bones every second.
- White blood cells called neutrophils last just 6 hours.

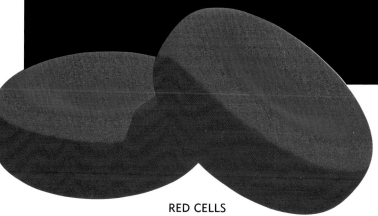

RED CELLS
Carry oxygen.

PLATELETS
Help blood to clot.

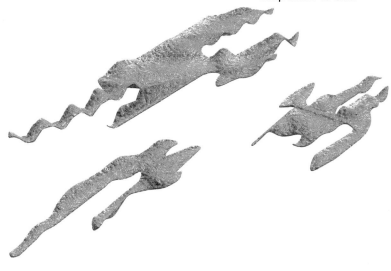

FOOD AND DIGESTION

ach of the body's cells is supplied with food in the form of small, simple molecules, carried in the blood. Yet the food we eat comes in solid lumps and liquids made up from large, complex molecules. So the body has its own food refinery, known as the digestive system, for breaking food down into the right molecules.

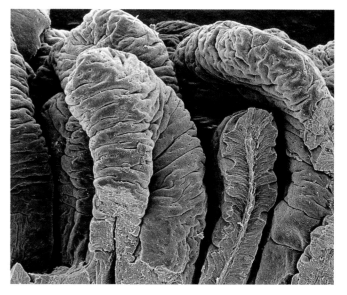

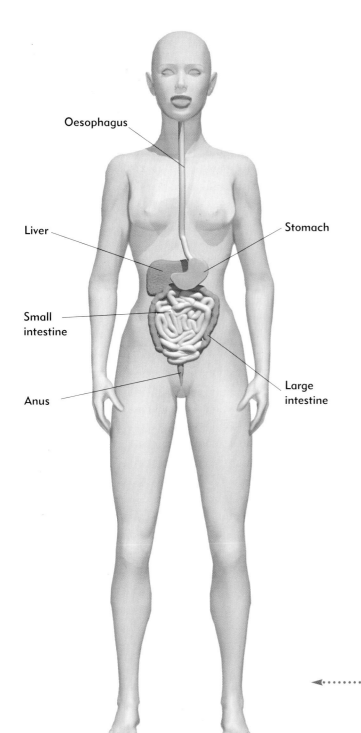

Oesophagus

Liver

Stomach

Small intestine

Anus

Large intestine

The microscope shows the intestines are lined with tiny folds that give a large area for absorbing digested food.

Your digestive system is a long tube winding through your body, called the alimentary canal. It starts from your mouth, runs down through your oesophagus (gullet), your stomach and a long coiled tube (your intestine) before finally ending at your anus. As food slowly passes through, it is gradually broken down into small molecules and absorbed into the bloodstream. Once absorbed, it is processed in the body's chemical refinery, the liver.

Breaking down Food

Digestion begins as soon as you put food in your mouth, as it is softened by chewing and by enzymes (chemical agents) in your saliva. But it is in your stomach that digestion begins in earnest. The stomach has strong, muscular walls. As soon as food enters, waves of squeezing and relaxation sweep across the stomach, churning and pounding the food. At the same time, glands in the stomach walls secrete 'gastric' juices, that start to dissolve the food chemically.

Most of the process of digestion takes place in the small intestine.

Into the Intestine

The stomach acts as a store for the partially digested food, letting it through gradually into the next stage of the canal, the intestine. When partially digested food passes into the intestine, it is in a semi-liquid mass called chyme. The gut is long and folded over and over again inside the abdomen. In the small intestine, chyme is broken down further still into the simple molecules that can be absorbed into the bloodstream and carried to the cells. Most digestion takes place in a section of the small intestine, called the **duodenum**, while most of the food is absorbed, or ingested, into the bloodstream in the ileum. Food that cannot be digested passes into the large intestine and is then expelled from the body through the anus.

The liver is the body's chemical factory, handling all the chemicals from digested food and preparing them for use in the body.

FACT FILE

HEALTHY DIET
Your diet is what you eat. A balanced diet includes the right amount of proteins, carbohydrates, fats, vitamins, minerals, fibre and water.
• Carbohydrates are foods made from kinds of sugar like glucose and starch and are found in foods such as bread, rice, potatoes and sweet things.
• Fats are oily foods. Some fats are solid like meat fats and cheese; some are liquid like cooking oil. Fats are essential to health and growth, and excess fats are stored around the body until needed.
• Proteins are needed to build and repair cells. Meat and fish are very high in protein but a vegetarian diet that includes eggs, milk and cheese provides all the essential acids.
• Fibre is plant fibres or 'roughage' that your body cannot digest but needs to keep the muscles of the bowel properly exercised.

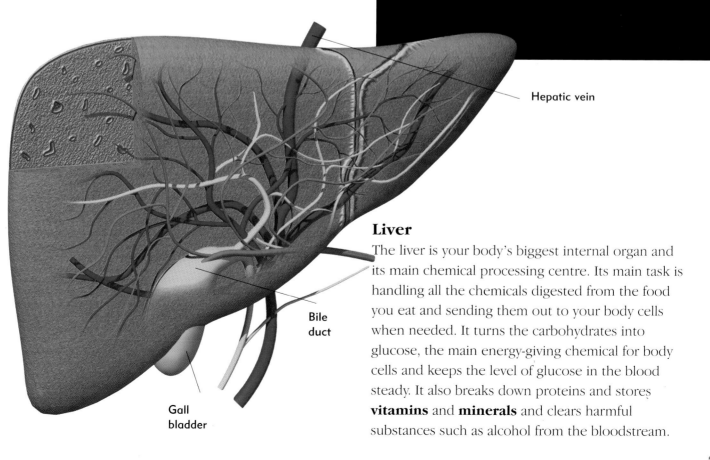

Hepatic vein

Bile duct

Gall bladder

Liver

The liver is your body's biggest internal organ and its main chemical processing centre. Its main task is handling all the chemicals digested from the food you eat and sending them out to your body cells when needed. It turns the carbohydrates into glucose, the main energy-giving chemical for body cells and keeps the level of glucose in the blood steady. It also breaks down proteins and stores **vitamins** and **minerals** and clears harmful substances such as alcohol from the bloodstream.

19

BODY FLUIDS

esides oxygen and food, your body needs one more vital input: water. You can live for more than a month without food but only a few days without water. If your body's water content goes up or down more than 5 per cent, it can kill you. Fortunately, your body is able to keep its water content remarkably steady, providing you drink enough.

Your body gains water in a number of ways – from what you eat and drink and as a by-product of the normal working of the cells. It loses water by sweating, breathing and urinating. Normally, the amount of water you gain from the cells and lose by breathing and sweating stays much the same. So your body controls water content mainly by balancing the water you drink against the water you lose by urinating.

When your body needs more water, a part of the brain called the **hypothalamus** makes you feel thirsty – so you drink water. The hypothalamus also sends out signals to another part of the brain called the **pituitary** which tells the kidneys to hold on to water. The hypothalamus works using special receptors.

In a sauna, the steamy atmosphere stops sweat evaporating, so your body goes on sweating to try and get cool.

 **FACT FILE**

Your body needs a regular intake of water.

WATER FACTS

Average water content of the body	60 per cent
Daily intake from drink	1.4 litres
Daily intake from food	0.8 litres
Daily water gain from body cells	0.3 litres
Average total daily water gain	2.5 litres
Daily loss from urine	1.5 litres
Daily loss from sweat	0.5 litres
Daily loss by vapour on breath	0.3 litres
Daily loss from in faeces	0.2 litres
Average daily water loss	2.5 litres
Water urinated during a lifetime	45,000 litres

These receptors constantly monitor the water in the blood. If the blood is too salty there must be too little water, so the hypothalamus makes you feel thirsty and makes your kidneys hold on to water. If the blood is not salty enough, the hypothalamus encourages you to urinate and lose water. This process occurs continually while you are awake but 'switches off' while you sleep.

The hypothalamus has 'volume' receptors as well as salt receptors. These measure the amount of blood – and so the amount of water – you have by detecting how much the walls of the heart and a few other blood vessels are stretched. If your blood volume drops, you immediately feel thirsty, and drink to restore the loss of water, which is why heavy bleeding makes you want to drink. In this way the volume of the water and the concentration of salt are precisely controlled.

Kidneys

Your two kidneys are your body's water control and blood-cleaning plants. They are high-speed filters that draw off water from the blood as it passes through, along with substances dissolved in it such as salt and vitamins. They feed the right amount of water and the right substances back into the blood and let the rest go as urine. All the body's blood flows through the kidneys every ten minutes, so blood is filtered 150 times a day.

Cutaway of a kidney. The kidneys are a pair of bean-shaped organs inside the small of your back. They sit in the path of your main arteries and veins, filtering out water and waste through millions of tiny filtration units called nephrons.

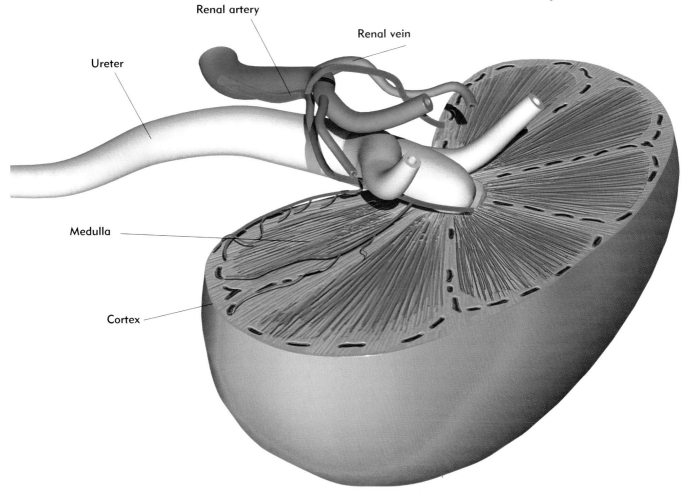

Renal artery

Renal vein

Ureter

Medulla

Cortex

SKELETON AND JOINTS

Your body is supported by a strong framework of bones called the skeleton. The skeleton provides an anchor for the muscles, supports the skin and other tissues, and protects your heart, brain and other organs. It is made up of over 200 rigid bones, joined together by softer, rubbery cartilage.

Bones are so strong that they will take twice as much squeezing as granite and can be stretched four times as much as concrete. Yet they are so light they only make up 14 per cent of your body's total weight. Weight for weight, bone is at least five times as strong as steel! Bone gets its strength from a unique combination of flexibility and stiffness. The flexibility comes from tough rope-like fibres of collagen. The word collagen comes from the Greek *kolla* meaning 'glue' and *gen* meaning 'forming' and it is collagen that holds the bone together. The rigidity comes from the hard mineral deposits that surround the collagen. Collagen is found throughout the body, but it is the combination of collagen and minerals, especially calcium, that makes bones so tough. Without calcium, bones would be as bendy as rubber; without collagen, they would be as brittle as biscuits.

Yet bones also owe some of their strength to their internal structure. In the long bones of the limbs, for instance, the shaft is not just solid bone. Under a tough coating, there is a compact mass of

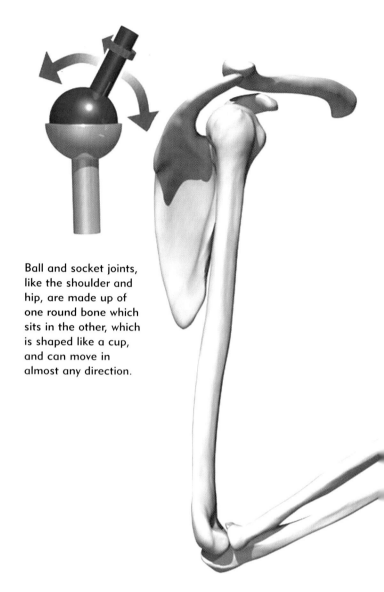

Ball and socket joints, like the shoulder and hip, are made up of one round bone which sits in the other, which is shaped like a cup, and can move in almost any direction.

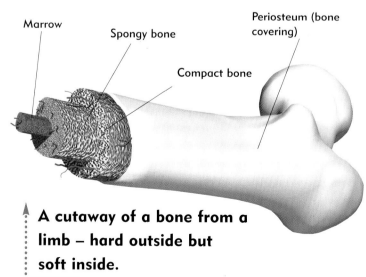

Marrow

Spongy bone

Periosteum (bone covering)

Compact bone

A cutaway of a bone from a limb – hard outside but soft inside.

interweaving rods called osteones. Deep inside the bone is the marrow, crisscrossed by tiny bone struts called trabeculae (spongy bone). Spongy bone also makes a strong but light internal structure at the head, or end of a long bone.

Bone Cells

The skeleton lasts longer than any other part of the body when we die. While we are alive, it is living, active tissue. In some parts of the bone, cells called osteoblasts are making new bone, but elsewhere cells called osteoclasts are breaking it down. These cells, or osteocytes, are surrounded by blood, just like any other cells.

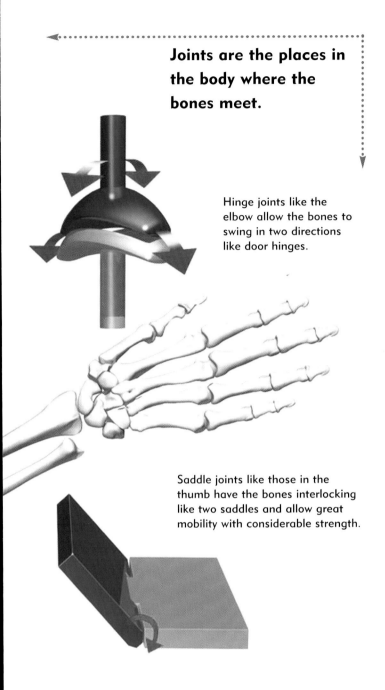

Joints are the places in the body where the bones meet.

Hinge joints like the elbow allow the bones to swing in two directions like door hinges.

Saddle joints like those in the thumb have the bones interlocking like two saddles and allow great mobility with considerable strength.

Osteocytes are found in a cavernous part of the bone, called lacunae. Sometimes osteocytes die, leaving empty lacunae to fill with salts which act as the body's mineral store.

The core of each bone is soft, jelly-like marrow. It can be red or yellow, depending on whether it has more blood or more fat. In bones with red marrow – such as the breastbone, ribs, shoulder blades and hips – the cells are even more active. Here millions of new red blood cells and white cells are being born every day. Yellow bone marrow is normally a store for fat, but it may turn to red marrow when you are ill, to help your body fight the illness.

FACT FILE

BONE COUNT

• An adult's skeleton has over 200 bones joined together by rubbery cartilage. Some adults have extra bones in the spine. A baby's skeleton has 300 or more bones but some of these fuse together as they grow older.

• A number of parts of the adult skeleton are fused together to make a single bone. The skull is fused from a variety of bones. The pelvis is made by fusing the ilium bone, the ischium bone (coccyx) and the pubis.

• The axial skeleton is the 87 bones of the upper body. It includes the skull, backbone, ribs and the breastbone. The appendicular skeleton is the 126 bones of the rest of the skeleton, essentially the arms and shoulders, legs and hips.

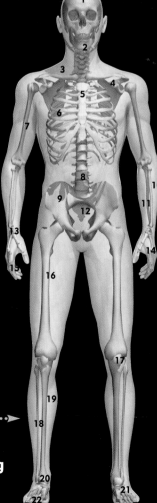

Key:
1. Skull
2. Jaw
3. Clavicle
4. Scapula
5. Sternum
6. Ribcage
7. Humerus
8. Vertebrae
9. Hip
10. Radius
11. Ulna
12. Pelvis
13. Carpels
14. Metacarpels
15. Phalanges (fingers)
16. Femur
17. Patella
18. Tibia
19. Fibula
20. Tarsals
21. Metatarsals
22. Phalanges (toes)

The skeleton is your body's living framework.

MUSCLES

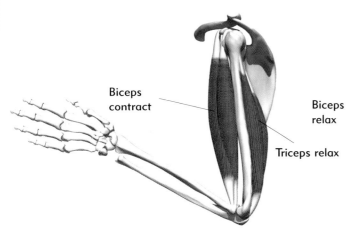

Biceps contract

Biceps relax

Triceps relax

The biceps muscles at the front of your upper arm contract to bend your arm. The triceps muscles at the back contract to straighten it.

Triceps contract

Muscle fibre

Stripes of actin and myosin

Myofibril

You need muscles to move any part of your body. You need muscles to move your leg. You need muscles to twitch an eyebrow. You even need muscles to sit still – for without muscles to hold the body upright, you would slump like a rag doll.

There are well over 600 muscles in the body under your control, each one a powerhouse of especially energetic cells. The sheer range of movements that muscles enable you to make seems almost infinite. Yet they all work simply by contracting and relaxing and just pulling two points together.

Most muscles are attached to bone either side of a joint, either directly or by a set of fibres called **tendons**, and simply pull the bones together as they contract.

Muscles can shorten themselves, but they cannot make themselves longer. Each time a muscle contracts, it must be pulled out again by another muscle. Muscles cannot 'push'.

Muscles are bundles of fibres made from lots of interlocking threads of actin and myosin.

Myosin filament

Skeletal muscles are anchored over your skeleton in two or three layers.

So muscles are typically in opposing pairs – a flexor muscle to bend or 'flex' a joint and an extensor muscle to straighten it. Not all muscles move things. Sometimes a muscle contracts just to hold parts of the body still and the muscle does not get any shorter.

How Muscle Works

Most muscles owe their power to a unique kind of cell. A muscle cell is one long fibre stretching from one end of the muscle to the other. Muscles are simply bundles of these fibres bound tightly together, like the strands of a telephone cable. Some muscles are made from just a few hundred fibres; others contain more than a quarter of a million. Just as each muscle is made from hundreds of long thin strands, so is each muscle fibre. The thin strands in muscle fibre are known as myofibrils.

Dark bands run round each myofibril. These bands line up so perfectly across the myofibrils that the whole muscle fibre looks stripy. Many muscles have another name: striated muscle, which means striped muscle. These stripes are really alternating bands of tiny filaments made of actin and myosin. Muscle gains its power to contract from the way the actin and myosin filaments interlock like fingers all the way along the fibril. When your brain sends the muscle a signal to contract, little buds on each of millions of myosin filaments twist sharply. As they twist, they drag the actin filaments along with them and pull the muscle shorter.

Types of Muscle

There are three kinds of muscle in the body: skeletal muscle, smooth muscle and cardiac muscle. Skeletal muscles are the muscles covering your body, the 'voluntary' muscles that you can control. Smooth muscles and cardiac muscles are involuntary, which means that they work entirely automatically.

TEST FILE

TIRED OUT?
Next time you play a sport, or do some other form of strenuous exercise, see if you can spot any signs of these changes in your body.
• The heart rate rises; the volume of blood pumped increases. (Test your pulse.)
• You breathe faster and deeper, taking in more air. (Count your breaths in a minute.)
• Blood vessels in the skin contract, diverting blood to active muscle. (How red are you?)
• Insulin levels drop, adrenalin rises so the liver makes more sugar available. (You may want to eat something sweet.)
• Your body temperature rises and you begin to sweat. The blood vessels in the skin dilate to lose heat. (You feel hot, and your skin is wet with sweat.)
• Lactic acid builds up in the muscles as they burn glucose without oxygen. (Your muscles feel sore.)
Are you fit? If so, all systems return to normal within minutes after light exercise. This is called 'recovery time'.

When muscles are exercised, they grow larger. At first, the fibres just grow thicker. But sustained training makes new fibres grow.

FITNESS

ike a car engine, muscles need fuel, and the fuel they use is glucose. Like all body cells, muscle cells get energy when glucose joins with oxygen in the process called cellular respiration (see page 12). This normal respiration may sometimes be called aerobic respiration because the oxygen comes indirectly from air. When you start exercising, sometimes your muscle cells burn up glucose and oxygen so fast the blood cannot deliver enough oxygen. So, for a while, the muscles burn glucose without oxygen. This is called anaerobic respiration which means respiration without air.

If you are fairly fit, your heart soon starts pumping blood faster and blood vessels open up to boost the oxygen supply and restore aerobic respiration. If you are unfit, your muscles go on working anaerobically for much longer.

When you are fit, your muscles work aerobically for most of the time.

Glucose combines with oxygen in a process called cellular respiration.

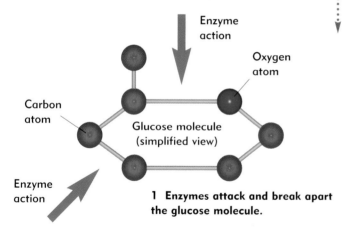

Carbon atom

Enzyme action

Oxygen atom

Glucose molecule (simplified view)

Enzyme action

1 Enzymes attack and break apart the glucose molecule.

This not only uses up glucose much, much more rapidly, tiring you out, but also leaves a build-up of lactic acid that makes overworked muscles feel sore. It is the body's efforts to draw in extra oxygen to burn off this acid that makes you pant when you stop running.

During a long race, the muscles of a fit athlete can work aerobically most of the time. But the supply of oxygen in the blood may not be enough for the final sprint to the finishing line. When the dash begins, the muscles switch over to anaerobic respiration, drawing on the last reserves of internal energy for the final burst of power.

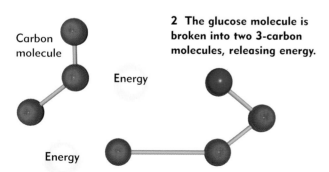

Carbon molecule

Energy

2 The glucose molecule is broken into two 3-carbon molecules, releasing energy.

Energy

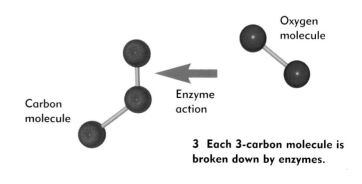

Oxygen molecule

Carbon molecule

Enzyme action

3 Each 3-carbon molecule is broken down by enzymes.

TEST FILE

GETTING FIT

If you do some strenuous exercise lasting at least 20 minutes, three or more times a week, you will gradually get more fit. Your body benefits from regular exercise in the following ways (you should be able to notice them as you become fitter):
- Your resting heart rate goes down.
- Your ability to pump extra blood quickly when needed improves.
- Your heart rate goes back to normal quicker after exercise.
- The muscles you exercise grow bigger.
- Your strength, stamina and endurance improve.
- Your ligaments and tendons become stronger.
- Your joints become more flexible.
- You lose excess weight if you exercise and eat a healthy diet.

Regular exercise builds up the body's ability to supply oxygen to the muscles.

In Training

Athletes build up their body's capacity to supply oxygen to muscles by aerobic exercise – exercise that lasts long enough for muscles to work aerobically. Their lungs grow larger, and their heart beats more strongly and slowly.

When muscles are exercised, they grow larger. At first the muscle fibres simply grow thicker. But continued regular training makes extra muscle fibres grow and the blood vessels supplying the muscle with oxygen grow more branches. So the muscles not only grow stronger but are better able to keep going. This only happens, though, if the exercise pushes them to 80 per cent of their capacity.

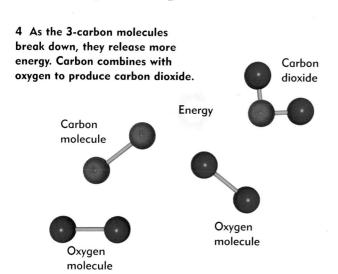

4 As the 3-carbon molecules break down, they release more energy. Carbon combines with oxygen to produce carbon dioxide.

Carbon dioxide

Energy

Carbon molecule

Oxygen molecule

Oxygen molecule

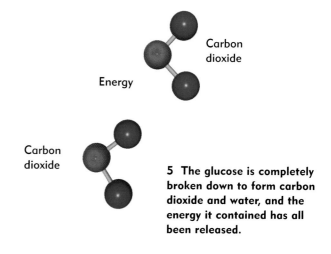

Carbon dioxide

Energy

Carbon dioxide

5 The glucose is completely broken down to form carbon dioxide and water, and the energy it contained has all been released.

NERVOUS SYSTEM

Your brain is linked to the rest of your body by an amazing network of nerves that are strung together like a tiny telephone network. It is continually alive with activity, buzzing little messages rapidly to and fro all over the body. Every second of the day, hundreds of nerve impulses arrive in the brain with information from the body's sense organs (eyes, ears and so on). Every second, just as many whizz out from the brain telling the sense organs what to do.

The focus of all this nerve activity is an amazing bundle of nerves running right down the backbone, called the **spinal cord**. This, together with the brain, makes up what is sometimes called the **Central Nervous System** (CNS). The CNS is the junction box of the nervous system, and every nerve message starts or finishes here.

This micrograph shows a nerve cell with its branching dendrites and axon.

Synapse

But spreading out from the CNS are hundreds upon hundreds of tiny thread-like nerves that stretch into all corners of the body. These form the Peripheral Nervous System (PNS).

Peripheral nerves carry messages both to and from the CNS, but each nerve can carry messages only one way. So the body has two types of nerve. First of all, there are nerves that feed information into the CNS from the body's sense receptors – touch, smell, taste, sight and hearing. These are called sensory nerves. Then there are nerves which rush instructions out from the CNS telling a muscle to contract or relax. These are called motor nerves because they prod muscles into motion.

Motor nerves to muscle

Each part of your body is controlled by two sets of nerves: sensory nerves which send back touch signals to the brain and motor nerves which tell muscles to move.

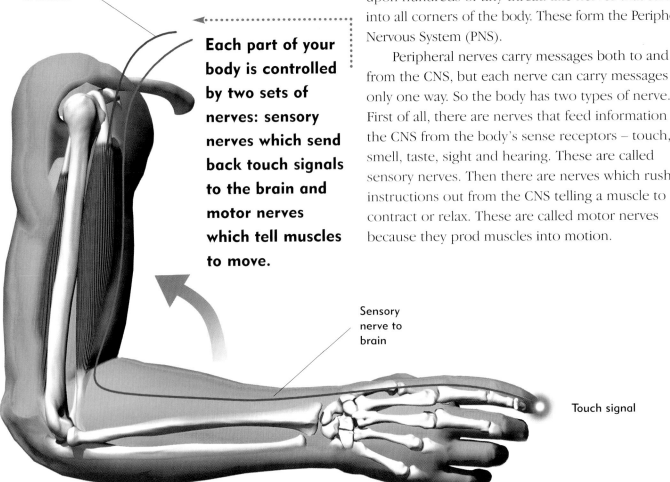

Sensory nerve to brain

Touch signal

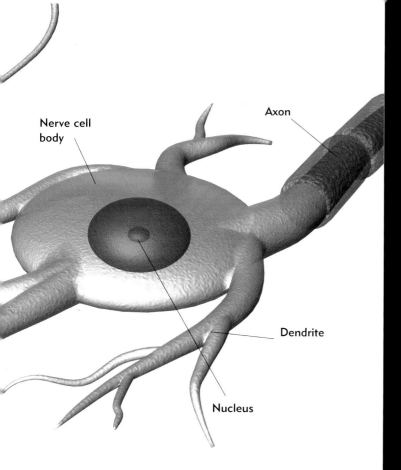

Nerve cell body

Axon

Dendrite

Nucleus

The nervous system is made from special cells called neurons.

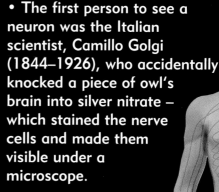

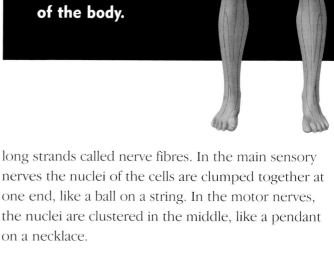

The nervous system is divided into the CNS – the brain and spinal cord, and the PNS which branches off to the rest of the body.

Nerve cells

Your nervous system is made up from long strings of nerve cells, called neurons, all linked together. Most body cells are quite short-lived, and are always being replaced by new ones. But neurons are very long-lived – which is a good thing, because after you are born, it is unlikely that any new ones will ever grow again!

In most cells, the nucleus and cell body form the greater part of the cell. But in nerve cells, the main body and nucleus are just a small part of the cell. Branching out from the main cell body are lots of tiny threads called dendrites and a long tail called an axon. Messages enter the neuron through the dendrites. They then rush along the axon. Near the far end, the axon splits into hundreds of feathery fibres that pass on the message to the dendrites of other nerve cells.

Most nerve cells are bundled together with others to make the major nerves of your nervous system, but they are bundled together in different ways. In the CNS, axons are bundled together in tangled bunches called interneurons. In the PNS, axons are bundled in long strands called nerve fibres. In the main sensory nerves the nuclei of the cells are clumped together at one end, like a ball on a string. In the motor nerves, the nuclei are clustered in the middle, like a pendant on a necklace.

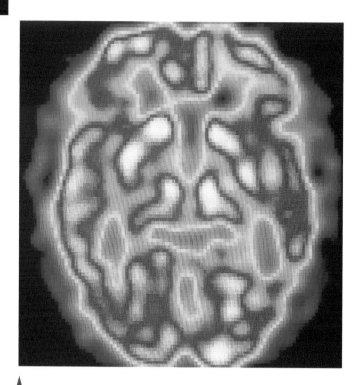

This scan shows the normal activity and functioning of the brain.

Inside your head you carry the most amazing structure in the universe: a human brain. It looks like little more than a gigantic, soft grey walnut with its wrinkled surface. But within this soft mass are billions of inter-linked nerve cells. The chemical and electrical impulses whizzing through all these cells create all your thoughts, record every sensation and control nearly all your actions. Every second of your life, your brain is receiving signals from the rest of your body and issuing instructions via the body's network of nerves. Even more amazingly, it lets you go on thinking, even when there are no inputs or outputs.

Your brain is made up from billions of neurons all linked together like an extraordinarily complicated computer. You can get an idea just how clever the human brain is compared with other animals by the number of neurons it has. The human brain has about 100 billion neurons. Insects have about 100,000 neurones while the tapeworm has just 162.

FACT FILE

BRAIN FACTS
• The human brain is made up of more than 100 billion nerve cells.
• Each neuron in the brain is connected to up to 25,000 other neurons, so there are trillions and trillions of possible pathways for nerve signals.
• Girls' brains weigh 2.5 per cent of their body weight; boys' brains weigh 2 per cent of their body weight (this does not affect the intelligence of the individual).
• The cortex of the human brain is four times as big as a chimp's, 20 times as big as monkey's and 300 times as big as a rat's.

Different areas of your brain are linked to different tasks. Some scientists call these association areas.

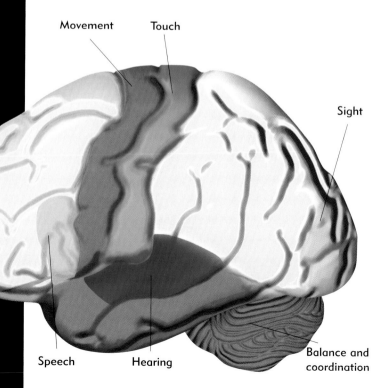

Movement   Touch

Sight

Speech   Hearing   Balance and coordination

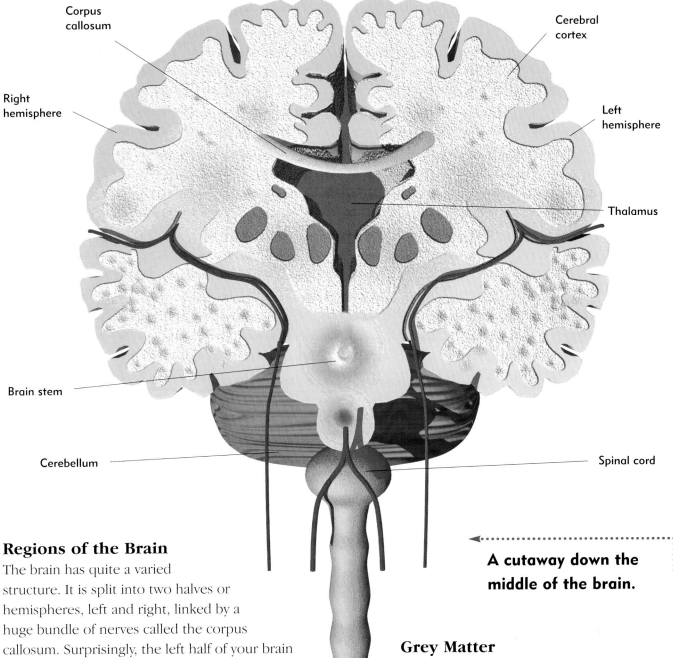

Corpus callosum

Cerebral cortex

Right hemisphere

Left hemisphere

Thalamus

Brain stem

Cerebellum

Spinal cord

► A cutaway down the middle of the brain.

Regions of the Brain

The brain has quite a varied structure. It is split into two halves or hemispheres, left and right, linked by a huge bundle of nerves called the corpus callosum. Surprisingly, the left half of your brain controls the right side of your body and vice versa.

Each side has three main regions. Deep in the centre, connected to the spinal cord, is the brain stem and the thalamus which sits on top of it. This is where basic functions like breathing and heart rate are controlled. The cerebellum is a plum-sized lump growing from the back of the stem which controls balance and coordination. Most of the brain, though, is the cerebrum, which wraps around the thalamus like a big cherry around a stone. This is where you think, and where complicated tasks like memory, speech and conscious control of movement go on.

Grey Matter

The outer surface of the cerebrum, like the rind on an orange, is the wrinkly bit on top of the brain. This is called the cerebral cortex or grey matter. This is where all the messages from the senses are received and where all the commands to the body to move come from. Even though it is no bigger than a bag of sugar, the brain's buzzing activity demands huge amounts of energy – and brain cells also depend on oxygen in the blood. If the blood supply to your brain were cut off, you would lose consciousness within ten seconds, and die within minutes.

SENSES

Your senses tell you about the world around you – its sights, sounds, its heat and cold and more. Even when you're asleep, your body is alive to sensations, both from inside and outside your body. There are five major senses – sight, hearing, smell, taste and touch – and your brain receives a constant stream of nerve signals from each of these senses, keeping your brain up-to-date with what is going on.

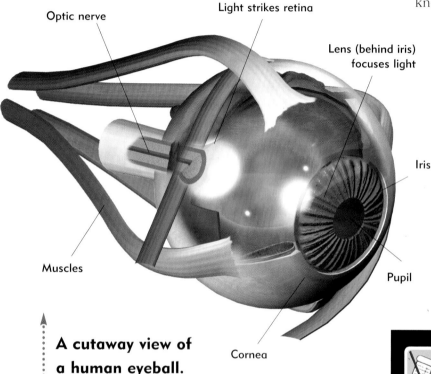

Optic nerve

Light strikes retina

Lens (behind iris) focuses light

Iris

Muscles

Pupil

Cornea

A cutaway view of a human eyeball.

Sight

Your eyes are two tough little balls filled with a jelly-like substance called vitreous humour. Each eyeball is a bit like a video camera. At the front is a lens (the pupil) – the dark spot in the middle of each eye. This projects a picture on to the lining of the back of the eye, called the retina. The retina is made up of millions of light-sensitive cells called rods and cones which transmit the picture to the brain via the optic nerve. Rods can pick up even very dim light, but cannot tell the difference between colours. Cones distinguish colours, but are not so sensitive to light as rods, which is why we do not see colours well at night. There are three kinds of cone, one sensitive to red light, one to blue and one to green.

Hearing

The flap of skin on the side of your head is only one part of the ear, called the outer ear, and simply funnels sound down a tube (the ear canal). Inside your head, in the middle ear, sounds hit a taut wall of skin called the eardrum, shaking it rapidly. As it shakes, it rattles three tiny bones or ossicles. Even further inside, in the inner ear, is a curly tube full of fluid called the cochlea. As the ossicles vibrate, they knock against this tube, making waves in the fluid. Minute hairs waggle in the waves, sending signals along nerves to the brain.

Smell

Smell seems to rely on a small patch of olfactory receptors inside the top of your nose. The olfactory receptors react to traces of different chemicals in the air. There are over five million of them and they need pick up only a few tiny molecules of a substance for you to identify a smell.

FACT FILE

SOUND FACTS

• Sound intensity is measured in decibels (db) which is a logarithmic scale – that is, three decibels are twice as loud as two, and four twice as loud as three.
• In the normal range of hearing you can hear sounds as deep as 20 Hertz (Hz) – vibrations a second – deeper than a bass drum, and sounds as high as 20,000 Hz.
• You can hear sounds as quiet as 10 db, which is quieter than leaves rustling in trees and as loud as 140 db or more, which is as loud as a jet engine close up.
• Sounds louder than 100 db can damage the ear.

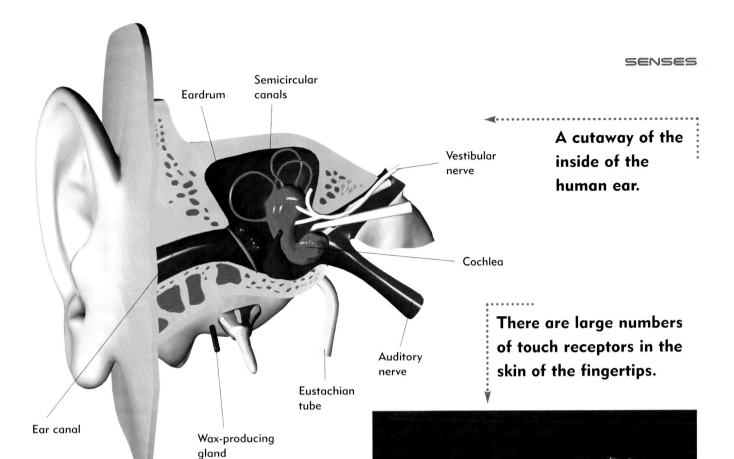

Eardrum

Semicircular canals

Vestibular nerve

Cochlea

Auditory nerve

Eustachian tube

Wax-producing gland

Ear canal

A cutaway of the inside of the human ear.

There are large numbers of touch receptors in the skin of the fingertips.

Taste

Taste is a mixture of different sensations, including smell. Your tongue has an array of different taste receptors called taste buds, which react to sweet, salty, bitter and sour tastes in food. Sweet detectors are commonest at the tip of the tongue, salty just behind on either side, sour and bitter further back.

The surface of the tongue magnified 80 times. The taste buds are located on the large, dark red 'papillae'.

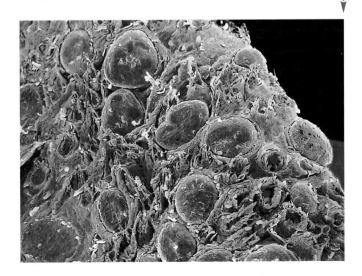

Touch

There are touch receptors all over the body. They react to four kinds of feeling – a light touch, steady pressure, heat and cold, and pain – and send a message to the brain via the nerves.

BODY CHEMICALS

Working hand in hand with the nervous system in controlling the body are chemical messengers called hormones. But while nerves transmit messages in a fraction of a second, hormones are carried in the bloodstream and deliver the message slowly. However, their effects tend to be more lasting and widespread. So while nerves are used when we need instant results, it is generally hormones that regulate the day-to-day running of the body.

The range of body processes controlled by hormones is vast. There are hormones to keep the body working steadily, such as anti-diuretic hormone (ADH), which helps the balance of water. There are hormones like adrenalin that boost the body to peak performance when needed. And there are hormones to regulate development, such as growth hormones, and sex hormones.

Hormones are tiny chemical molecules, each with a particular shape. The shape is crucial, for a hormone's shape is not only its identity card but its message. Hormones work by changing the internal chemistry of individual cells. Each hormone must deliver its message to the right series of cells, called its target cells. For some hormones, the target cells

The thrill of a rollercoaster brings a rush of the hormone adrenalin which makes your heart beat faster, your eyes widen and your body sweat.

may be just one specific type of cell. Other hormones work on every cell in the body. Each target cell has special receptor sites that can recognize the right hormone by its shape. So as the hormones are washed past in the bloodstream, they slot into the receptors in or on their target cells like a key into a lock.

Many smaller hormone molecules can slip through cell walls and link up directly with receptors floating inside the target cell. But many larger hormone molecules, such as adrenalin, link up with receptors on the cell surface. As the hormone arrives, a second chemical messenger – usually cyclic AMP – sets off inside the cell to pass on the news to the chemical that will set events in motion. It is as if the hormone is the postal worker delivering a letter, while cyclic AMP is the receptionist taking the letter in to the manager of the works.

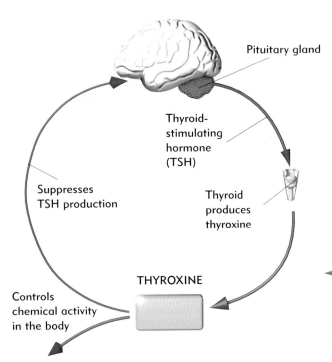

Pituitary gland

Thyroid-stimulating hormone (TSH)

Suppresses TSH production

Thyroid produces thyroxine

THYROXINE

Controls chemical activity in the body

The thyroid gland is stimulated to produce thyroxin which speeds up chemical reactions in the body.

Endocrine Hormones

Many of the body's hormones are made in special glands next to major blood vessels. These glands are called endocrine glands, and hormone control is often known as the endocrine system. Each gland secretes a different set of hormones – the thyroid gland in the neck, for instance, controls how fast we burn our food with its hormone thyroxine. The nearby parathyroid gland secretes a hormone that balances levels of calcium in the body.

Endocrine glands.

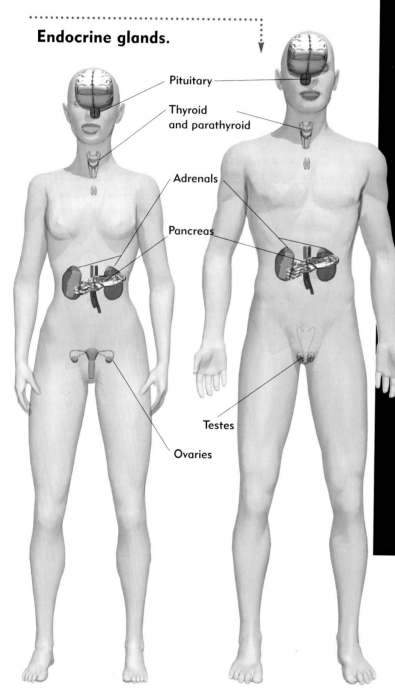

Pituitary

Thyroid and parathyroid

Adrenals

Pancreas

Testes

Ovaries

FACT FILE

HORMONES

Brain
• Endorphins and enkephalins (body chemicals) reduce pain.

Pituitary gland
• Growth hormone spurs growth and cell activity.
• Thyroid stimulating hormone (TSH) stimulates the thyroid which controls how fast you burn food.
• Anti-diuretic hormone (ADH) tells the kidneys to cut urine production.
• Follicle-stimulating hormone (FSH) and luteinizing hormone (LH) stimulate ovaries in females. LH affects the testes to produce androgens in males.

Thyroid
• Thyroid hormone raises cell activity.
• Calcitonin controls levels of calcium in the blood.

Thymus
• Makes hormones that produce white blood cells that defend against disease.

Adrenal glands
• Adrenalin and noradrenalin set off fight or flight response.

Pancreas
• Insulin and glucagon control blood-sugar levels.

Ovaries
• Oestrogen and progesterone control the menstrual cycle.

Testes
• Testosterone affects male sex organs producing male characteristics.

The pituitary gland is the key to the whole system. This tiny, pea-sized gland in the head sends out a range of hormones just like any other gland. But it also releases special 'tropic' hormones that coordinate the release of hormones from many other glands.

GROWING AND CHANGING

Your body starts growing bigger from the very moment you are conceived, and then goes on growing until you are in your late teens. Typically, children grow faster in the first few years, then grow slower, then go through a growth spurt in their early teenage years. But different children grow at different rates.

Girls grow faster at some stages while boys grow faster at others. Baby boys grow faster than baby girls – but only for the first seven months, then girls begin to shoot ahead until about the age of four. After that girls and boys grow at the same rate until puberty. Girls reach puberty first so grow taller than boys for a while. Finally, boys reach puberty and grow taller.

As you grow, you don't simply get taller and heavier. Different parts of your body grow at different rates, so you actually change shape. When you are born, your head is already three-quarters the size it is going to be when you are adult, and by the time you are one year old, it is almost full adult size. So your head appears to shrink as you grow older, while your legs are relatively longer.

Puberty

You are born with reproductive or sexual organs, but they only develop in the right way for you to have children once you reach the age of puberty – typically when you are 11 to 13 years old. At puberty, hormones sent out by the pituitary gland (see page 35) flood through your body, stimulating the changes that turn boys into men and girls into women. When a girl reaches puberty, she begins to grow breasts, and soft, downy hair sprouts under her arms and around her genitals (pubic hair). Soon her hips begin to grow wider and her waist slimmer. Eventually, she begins her monthly periods, or menstruation. When a boy reaches puberty, his testes grow and change shape, and begin to produce sperm. At the same time, he begins to grow pubic hair and hair on his chin.

As you grow, you body changes its shape.

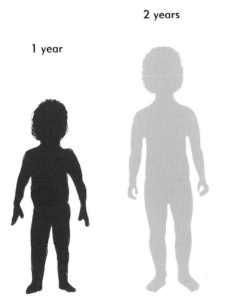

1 year

2 years

6 years

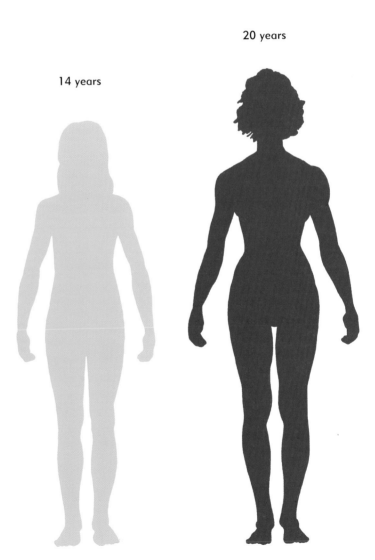

14 years

20 years

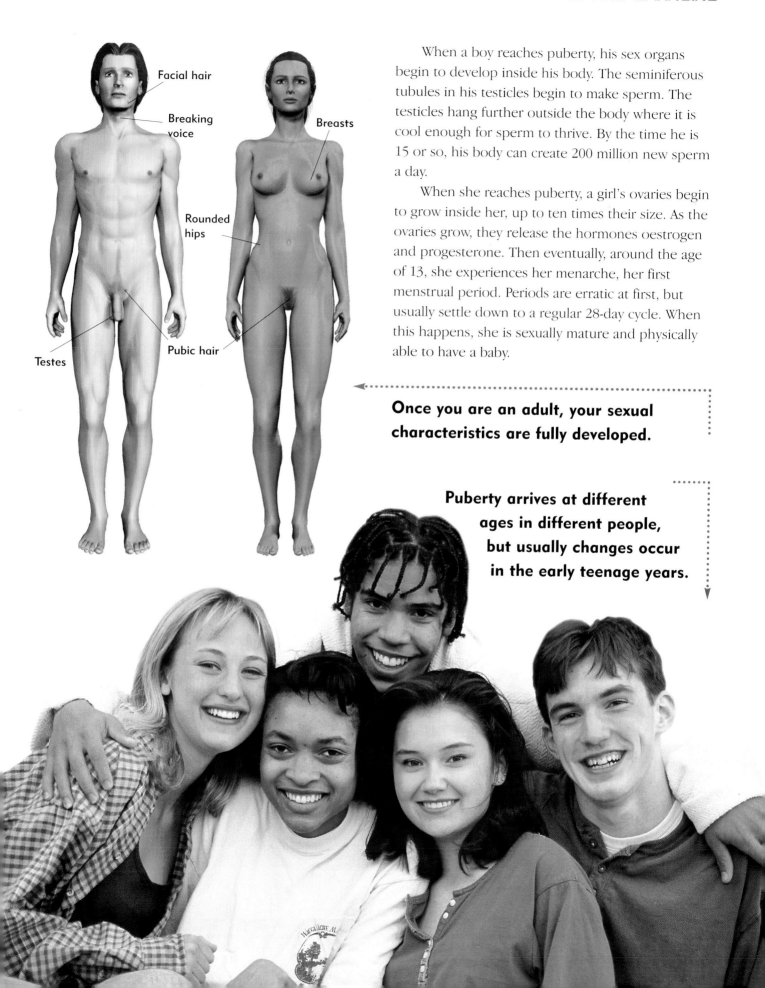

Facial hair

Breaking voice

Breasts

Rounded hips

Pubic hair

Testes

When a boy reaches puberty, his sex organs begin to develop inside his body. The seminiferous tubules in his testicles begin to make sperm. The testicles hang further outside the body where it is cool enough for sperm to thrive. By the time he is 15 or so, his body can create 200 million new sperm a day.

When she reaches puberty, a girl's ovaries begin to grow inside her, up to ten times their size. As the ovaries grow, they release the hormones oestrogen and progesterone. Then eventually, around the age of 13, she experiences her menarche, her first menstrual period. Periods are erratic at first, but usually settle down to a regular 28-day cycle. When this happens, she is sexually mature and physically able to have a baby.

Once you are an adult, your sexual characteristics are fully developed.

Puberty arrives at different ages in different people, but usually changes occur in the early teenage years.

MALE AND FEMALE

Every 28 days or so, a woman's body goes through a regular cycle of changes called the menstrual cycle. They affect the whole body, but their purpose is to prepare one of the woman's eggs or ova for fertilization. Only a few eggs are ever fertilized, so the cycle normally ends with the shedding of the egg and other preparations, ready for a fresh start next month.

Unlike male sperm, female sex cells (called oocytes) are ready formed at birth. Each of these cells is held in a little bag or follicle in the woman's ovary. By the time a girl reaches puberty, there may be half a million follicles still left in the ovaries, but far fewer ever become ova (eggs). The menstrual cycle starts when the pituitary gland in the brain (see page 35) sends out follicle-stimulating hormone (FSH) and prods half a dozen dormant follicles to start growing. As the follicles grow, they begin to secrete another hormone – the sex hormone oestrogen.

Oestrogen spurs the lining of the **uterus** to thicken into a rich bed called the endometrium, ready for the fertilized egg. It also, eventually, triggers the pituitary gland to send out luteinizing hormone (LH).

Ovulation and Menstruation

One follicle grows much bigger than the others, and after 14 days becomes a mature Graafian follicle. When LH reaches the ovary, then the follicle bursts from its sac, releasing the egg or ovum, which slides down the Fallopian tube towards the uterus. This is called ovulation. The abandoned follicle turns from white to yellow to become a corpus luteum

A new life begins when a single male sperm penetrates the female egg (ovary) to fertilize it.

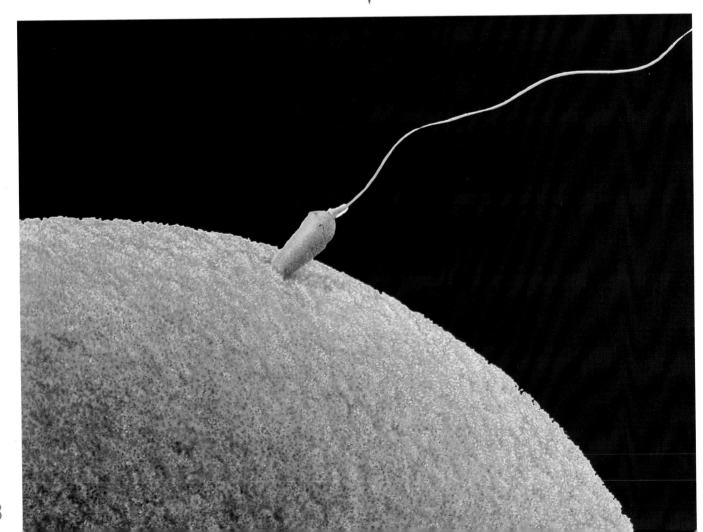

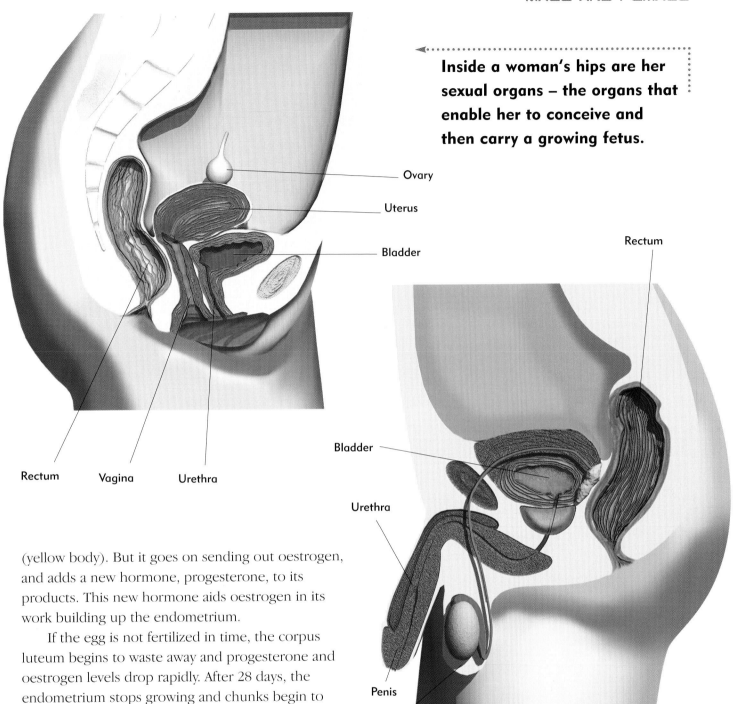

Ovary

Uterus

Bladder

Rectum

Rectum   Vagina   Urethra

Bladder

Urethra

Penis

Testicle

Inside a woman's hips are her sexual organs – the organs that enable her to conceive and then carry a growing fetus.

(yellow body). But it goes on sending out oestrogen, and adds a new hormone, progesterone, to its products. This new hormone aids oestrogen in its work building up the endometrium.

If the egg is not fertilized in time, the corpus luteum begins to waste away and progesterone and oestrogen levels drop rapidly. After 28 days, the endometrium stops growing and chunks begin to break off, releasing blood, fluids, mucus and fragments of uterine lining. The remnants of the endometrium flood out through the vagina as menstrual flow called a 'period'. After about five days of menstrual flow, FSH is released from the pituitary and the cycle begins over again.

If, by any chance, the egg is fertilized by sperm, the corpus luteum goes on growing and secretes more progesterone and oestrogen. The two hormones help to make the endometrium more and more thick and spongy, ready for the egg. Soon the fertilized egg will plant itself in the wall of the uterus.

A man's sexual organs are on the inside and outside of his body. They enable him to produce sperm and father a child.

Long after the egg has settled in and begun to develop, the corpus luteum will go on sending out progesterone to thicken the endometrium and provide plenty of nourishment through pregnancy.

NEW LIFE

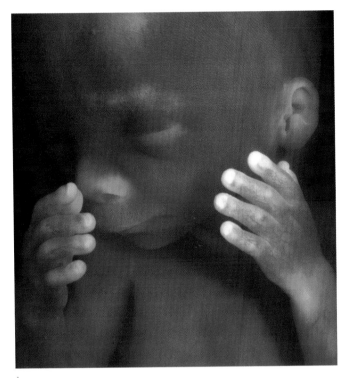

A male fetus developing in its mother's womb, at about 19 weeks.

Mitosis is the way cells divide to create new cells when you are growing to replace those that have worn out. Each new cell gets an identical copy of the original cell's chromosomes.

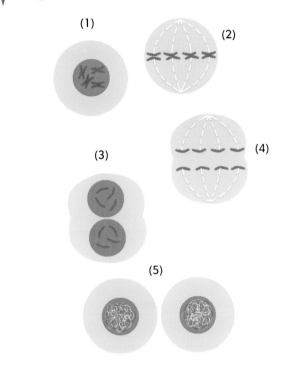

(1) Before the cell divides, each chromosome is copied to make X-shaped pairs.

(2) The chromosome pairs are drawn into a line across the centre of the cell.

(3) The pairs of chromosomes separate and each half is pulled along threads to opposite ends of the cell.

(4) Two little bags or nuclei form round the chromosomes clustered at each end.

(5) Eventually mitosis is completed as the cell splits in two between the nuclei.

New cells are being made in your body all the time to help you grow or replace any cells that are damaged or reach the end of their natural lifespan. Red blood cells rarely live long, for instance, but every second 1.5 million new ones are being made in your bones to replace them. All these new cells are made as cells called stem cells split in half to make two new cells, which then split in half again and again to make more cells in a process called mitosis.

Inside the nucleus of each cell in your body are 46 microscopically tiny, twisted threads called chromosomes, each made of a remarkable chemical called DNA. The DNA in the chromosomes provides the cell's complete instructions for life in a chemical code in millions of instalments called genes. When cells split, each of the new cells must be identical and carry the same set of instructions. So before each cell divides, it makes a copy of the DNA in its chromosomes to share between the two new cells in a process called replication.

There are actually two sets of chromosomes in each of your body cells – 23 from your mother and 23 from your father. So before your life began, both your father's and mother's bodies had to make special germ cells with just one set of chromosomes in a special cell division process called meiosis.

Meiosis is how cells split to create special germ cells. Germ cells have half the normal number of chromosomes (23 instead of 46) and combine with another germ cell to start a new life.

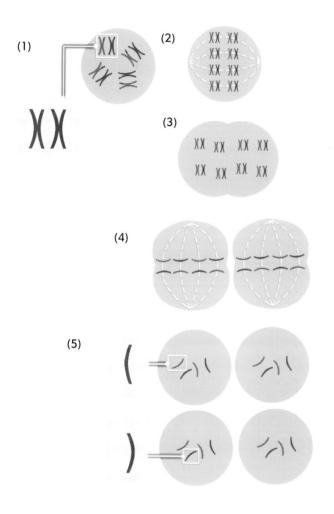

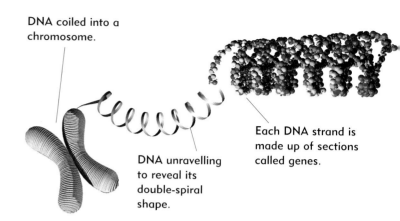

DNA coiled into a chromosome.

DNA unravelling to reveal its double-spiral shape.

Each DNA strand is made up of sections called genes.

DNA is the remarkable double-spiral shaped chemical molecule inside every body cell. It carries instructions both for the cell's activities and for a complete new human.

(1) Before cell division begins, each chromosome is copied to make X-shaped pairs and then they swap over genes.

(2) The chromosome pairs are drawn into a line across the centre of the cell.

(3) The pairs of chromosomes separate, as in mitosis, to leave two cells with the normal number of chromosomes.

(4) The chromosome pairs line up across the middle of each of the two new cells, then separate and are tugged to the ends of the cells.

(5) The two new cells then split but because there has been no copying of chromosomes, each of the four new cells is a germ cell with a half set of chromosomes.

Fertilization

Your life began when a germ cell from your father (the sperm) joined with a germ cell from your mother (the egg or ovum). This is called fertilization. Fertilization normally occurs during sexual intercourse between a man and a woman. At the climax of intercourse, millions of tiny sperm shoot out of the man's penis into the woman's vagina. The sperms then swim up the woman's uterus towards her Fallopian tubes, where an egg may be waiting. Very few sperm make contact with an egg, but only one is needed to fertilize and start a new life growing inside a woman.

The moment a sperm fertilizes an egg, the woman becomes pregnant and the new life begins to develop inside her. The egg begins to divide by mitosis to make more cells and grows into what is called an embryo. After eight weeks, the embryo develops into a fetus. Unlike an embryo, a fetus has stubby arms and legs and internal organs like a heart. The fetus grows rapidly inside the woman's uterus, now called a womb – and the womb grows with the fetus. After nine months, the fetus is fully grown and ready to be born as a baby.

STAYING HEALTHY

The world is full of billions of microscopic organisms including viruses, bacteria and various other microbes. They are in the air, in food, in water, on surfaces – in fact, just about everywhere. There are even microbes living inside your body. Most are completely harmless, such as the *E. coli* bacteria which lives in your intestine. But every now and then damaging microbes get inside your body and make you ill by releasing toxins or interrupting the body's normal activities. Any microbe that is harmful is called a pathogen – or 'germ'. When a colony of pathogens begins to multiply inside your body, you are suffering from an infectious disease.

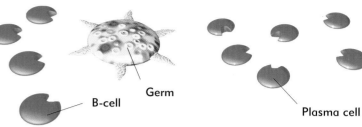

B-cell

Germ

Plasma cell

1a. A B-cell finds and makes contact with a germ, identified by matching proteins on its surface.

1b. B-cell multiplies forming versions of itself called plasma cells.

The Body's Defences

Fortunately your body has an array of defences to guard against germs but if the germs get past the defences, there is a formidable arsenal of weapons to fight them off. In the blood, for instance, there is a mixture of liquid proteins called complement, which is activated by bacteria and attacks them. There are also proteins called interferons which attack viruses. But the main weapons in the body's **immune system** are a range of white blood cells.

Phagocytes and Lymphocytes

First of all, there are the big 'eating cells' or phagocytes, which swallow up germs like vacuum cleaners then digest them with **enzymes**.

FACT FILE

IMMUNIZATION
Immunization helps protect you against an infectious disease by exposing you to a mild or dead version of a germ to help your body build up antibodies. In many countries, a series of vaccinations are given to protect you against certain diseases. This is a typical programme for the under 5s:
• Diphtheria, whooping cough and tetanus in a combined injection, plus polio in a sugar lump (at 3 months, 5 months and 9 months).
• Measles, mumps and German measles in a combined injection, plus polio in a sugar lump (at 15 months).
• Diphtheria, whooping cough and tetanus in a combined injection, plus polio in a sugar lump (at 4–5 years).

A group of children in Ghana are vaccinated against tetanus.

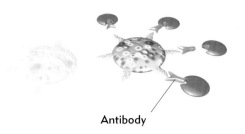

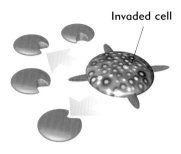

Invaded cell

Antibody

1c. Plasma cells make antibodies to attack the germ. They lock on to the germ so it can be eaten by phagocytes.

1d. B-cells multiply after the germ has been cleared in case of further attack.

2a. A cell invaded by a virus is identified by abnormal proteins on its surface.

This sequence of illustrations shows how the body's defences attack and kill germs (1a–1d) and body cells that have been invaded by viruses (2a–2d).

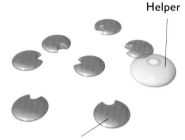

Helper

2b. Helper cells meet these proteins and chemicals tell killer cells to multiply.

Killer cell

Lymphocytes help target particular invaders by the work of T-cells and B-cells. T-cells work against viruses and other microbes that hide inside body cells. Helper T-cells identify such invaded cells and send out chemical alarms. Killer cells lock on to the identified cells and destroy them. B-cells use antibodies to target bacteria. There are thousands of different B-cells in the blood, and each has antibodies against a certain germ. Normally there are only a few B-cells with each antibody, but when a germ is detected, the right B-cell multiplies rapidly and releases floods of antibodies.

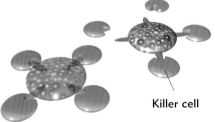

2c. Killer cells lock on to an abnormal cell and destroy it.

Killer cell

Antibodies

The body is armed from birth with antibodies for germs it has never met. This is called 'innate' immunity. If the body encounters a germ it has no antibodies for, it quickly makes some – and leaves 'memory' cells ready to be activated should the germ invade again. This is called 'acquired' immunity. Acquired immunity means you only suffer once from some infections, like chickenpox. **Immunization** (vaccination) works by triggering this system.

2d. Killer cells wait in case of attack by further abnormal cells.

A lymphocyte (blue) attacks and swallows an invading yeast cell.

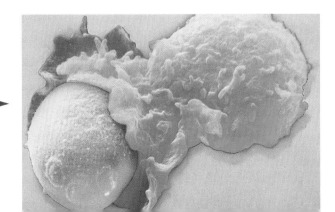

Cartilage A tough rubbery substance present in places in the body where bone would be too stiff – in your nose, for instance, and to cushion joints between bones.

Central Nervous System The nerves that make up the brain and the spinal cord. This is the body's control centre.

Duodenum Part of the small intestine next to the stomach.

Enzyme A chemical substance needed to make some processes occur, or speed them up. Digestion relies on enzymes that help break down the food.

Haemoglobin Oxygen-carrying substance in the red blood cells.

Hypothalamus Region of the brain that controls things like body temperature, thirst and hunger.

Immune system Your body's array of defences against microscopic invaders such as germs. It includes physical barriers such as the skin and mucus and chemical weapons such as white blood cells.

Immunization A way of protecting your body against disease in the future using its immune system. It works by exposing your body to a safe version of the disease to enable your body to build up its defences.

Neuron Nerve cell, made up of a central nucleus, a long transmitting tail called the axon, and branching receiving 'aerials' called dendrites.

Pituitary A small ductless gland at the base of the brain.

Respiration The chemical process in which food is broken down in cells using oxygen to release energy.

Spinal cord The bundle of nerves running down through the backbone from which all nerves radiate to the rest of the body.

Tendons Tough fibrous tissues connecting muscle to bone.

Uterus The place in a woman's body where a baby can grow. When a woman is pregnant, the uterus is called the womb.

Vitamins and **minerals** Substances that you must have in your food in small quantities for various vital body processes.

ORGANIZATION TO CONTACT

Science Museum

Exhibition Road, South Kensington, London SW7 2DD, UK. Tel. 020 7942 4000
Technological and medical changes over hundreds of years: includes anatomy, anaesthetics, nursing and hospitals, psychology, public health and much more. Also includes the medical collections of Sir Henry Wellcome.

BOOKS TO READ

The Complete Book of the Brain by John Farndon (Hodder Wayland, 2000)
The Concise Encyclopedia of the Body by David Burnie (Dorling Kindersley, 1994)
The Human Body Explained by Philip Whitfield (Hamlyn, 1995)
How the Body Works by Steve Parker (Dorling Kindersley, 1994)
Incredible Body illustrated by Stephen Biesty (Dorling Kindersley, 1997)
1000 Things you should know about the Human Body by John Farndon (Miles Kelly, 2000)

CD-ROMS

Become a Human Body Explorer (Dorling Kindersley, 1999)
The Magic School Bus Human Body (Scholastic, 1998)

WEB SITES

http://www.yucky.kids.discovery.com/flash/body
Through the characters of Wendell the Worm and Dora, this site gives a lighthearted view of various body functions.

http://www.kidshealth.org/kid/
A site introducing all kinds of health issues and focusing on how the body works.

http://www.innerbody.com/htm/body.html
A site exploring the human body through ten of the basic systems.

INDEX

How We See

Each of your eyes is a like a video camera. At the front is a lens called the cornea. This is the domed centre of each eye. This projects a picture on to the retina at the back of the eye. The retina is made up of millions of light-sensitive cells called rods and cones. These send the picture to the brain via the optic nerve. Rods pick up dim light but cannot distinguish colours. Cones detect colour and detail but only in bright light.

The sclera is the eye's tough but soft outer shell.

The picture of the body is projected upside down on the retina.

The retina is covered in millions of light-sensitive rods and cones.

The iris alters the size of the pupil to control how much light enters the eye.

The cornea, the eye's main lens, projects the the picture through the lens into the eye.

Light rays travel from the real object into the eye.

The original real object seen by the eye.

The pupil is the dark window that lets light into the eye.

The lens helps to focus the picture inside the eye.

The eyeball is filled with a jelly-like substance called vitreous humour.

The optic nerve transports the picture signals to the brain.